Crip Chronicles

"Gang Culture of South Central
Mega of Street Gang Warfare"

HOLY
BIBLE

ANGELO WHITE

This is a work of non-fiction, written from the author's memory. Some details may not align with other persons' memory of shared events, but the author shares the events from his memory.

CLF Publishing, LLC.
www.clfpublishing.org

ISBN #978-1-945102-43-1

Cover design by Senir Design. Contact information: info@senirdesign.com.

Printed and manufactured in the United States of America

Dedications

This book is dedicated to the following people:

Louis Angelo, White Jr. Lanique Cheyanne White, Sky D'Angelo White, King White, Angelo Louis White, T. Manuel, Raymond Lee Washington, Sr., Stanley "Big Tookie" Williams, *First Lady* Bonnie Williams, O'Neal Brown, Jr., Hebrew-Yahshua: Magnificent, Terry Carney, AKA Big T', Brother Charles Jackson, Donald Goines* Dr. Ron Karenga, Charles A. White, Iva Jean Burton White, Dorthy Burton Powell AKA Aunt Chic', Elizabeth Burton Young AKA Aunt Belle*, Gracie Mae Clark Burton, Charles N. Burton White, Isle Burton, Dr. V.G. Mc Guinness, Youth Kufu Instructor Charles Murphy, Charles Edward Burton 'Uncle Charlie', Sgt. Robert Jones, Riccardo Sims, Bulb, Conrad Williams, Melvin L. Hardy, Sr. Curtis Marrow, 'Buddha' Michael Harrison, Michael 'Thank U' Concepcion, Louis Concepcion, Vincent Concepcion, Michelle Concepcion Johnson, Nunu Brenda Concepcion, Kevin Sylvester *Good Buddy, Fred Hampton, Jr., Daryll Tolbert *TD, Michael Johnson, Melvin Johnson, Den Den Johnson, Hurc & Deadeye Heplin, Bobby Rosser *Priest, Michael & Junior Orwine, Willy Johnson *Monkeyman, Winnetka Vaden, Taco Owens, Chuckie-Todd-Anthony Madison, Bunche Griffin, Chico Bell, Willie Gather, Eddie Hawthorne, Gary-Michael Lewis, David Clark, Kinney Young. Michael & Rita Steel, Desmond & Barbara Washington, Ronald H. Young, Sr. & Jr. Rhonda Young, Carl Young, Gary Young, Bobby Williams, Sr. & Jr., Bull & Box Bulloc's & Family, Larry Mosley, Dregory Paulk, James-Elain-Hawk Anthony Young, Bebe Hardy, Bertha Hardy, Leroy Hardy, Mr. & Mrs. Moody Family Donald-Daryll- D'wynn-Denise, Roy Jones, Kerry Riley, Mice-Cutes-Rusty-Frank Bells, Keith-Ricky Hendersons, Michael Christian AKA Pretty Pretty Iron Dolimike, Leon Watson, Carl Mosier, Cody Brown Sr. & Jr. -Kerry Brown, Rodney Jones, Allan Ennis, James Lee, Steven Henderson AKA Chopper, Cliff Fowler AKA Fat Albert, Erskine Jones AKA OG Mad Dogg, W.C., Ice Cube, Long Beach Snoop Dogg, Ice T, Carl Ross, Jr. AKA Buster, Barry Campell, Wendel Warren AKA Maxie, Michelle-Herman Moncrief, Squally Davis, and David Dukes.

Acknowledgements

Yahshua John 5:43-47

Kev Mac "Allhood Magizine," Brother Charles Jackson, Otis Smith, Darla Hardy Rideaux, Wanda Hardy, Carlos A. White, Peaka's Winbush, V.G Mcginnis, Fitzgerald Godwin AKA Poo, Brenda Session, Perry T. Manuel, Louis Concepcion, Michael Concepcion, Vincent Concepcion, Vincent Samuel, Bunche Griffin, Willy Johnson AKA Monkey Man, Kevin Sylvester AKA Good Buddy, Big Fly, Lil Fly, Mr. & Mrs. Desmond Washington, Stanley & Bonny Williams, Mr. & Mrs. Curtis Brown, Sr., Kayso & Mrs. Robinson, Mr. Michael Christian AKA Pretty Pretty Iron Dolimike, Mr. & Mrs. Armerlin, Mr. & Mrs. O'Neal, Sr. & Mrs. Brown, Mr. & Mrs. Armours, Mr. & Mrs. Curtis-Gladys Brown, Sr. Leroy & Martha Hardy, Charles & Mrs. Moody, The Hatcher Family, Conrad & Eric Williams, Ronald & Johnny Burnett, Mr. & Mrs. Butlers, Brenda & Pat Lockhearts, Sgt. Robert Jones, Michael & Rita Steels, The Youngs Family, Murice AKA Moe, OD Shaw, OD Gilchest, Ricky & Keith Henderson, Tony Sims AKA Big Lurch, Nathan Price, Charles Manuel, Dorthy Powell AKA Aunt Chic', Elizabet Burton Young, Iva Jean Burton White, Johnny O'Qinn, Nelvin Hardy, Curtis Marrow, Bebe Hardy, Bede Powdrill, Shon & Sheila Sims, Steven Henderson AKA Big Chopper, Terrence & Mark Gibson AKA Stoney, Charles Murphy, Nathan & Wynn Cook, Johnny Rae Johnson, Odell Shaw, Lupe, Poochie, The Strawberries Family, Jeromie Otey AKA Bgjay-7 Moomoo Jones, Eskin, Jones AKA Mad-Dog, Joe Ransom, Roy Jones, T'Bone, Darryl Fisher, Michael Thomas, Louie Tenant, Blacc Ant, Blueboy, Blacc Dog, Ice Cube, Bubba Loc Hill, Fred Hill AKA OOOG Snoopdogg, Boo Manuel, Big U, Michael & A.C. Harrison. Big Bob, Fred Hampton, Jr. Donald Achie AKA Sweet Bacc, Riccardo Sims AKA Bulb, James Cumminham AKA Cuzz, Mice' Bell, Rusty Bell, Frank Bell, Cues' Bell, Dartanion, Shorty Fierson, Buster Cole, Carl Vernon AKA Mr. X, Jimmy Johnson, The Bullock Family, Bitterdog Bruno, Gerald AKA Peepee, C.Dog, Priest, Keith Reese, Allen Reed, Vincint Sammuel, Charles Mahaley, Allen Reed, Wilbur And Joesphine Armerlin, Pamela-Kim Armerlin. Darrell Armerlin, Mickey & Michael Cannllas, David McKinnan AKA Mumbles, Charles-Jackie Watsons, Ellis Jr., Qually Davis, Kim Elan, Darryl Butler, Angie Hamilton, Archie Crump. Anthony Young, Rainbow Young, Ben-Taco, Craig Craddock, Raymond Lee Washington Sr., Stanley "Big Tookie" Williams, Donald Foster, Diron Family, Cheateau Family, Red Isreal, Dave Cathey, Sammuel Carr, Jr., Sam Carr, Jr. Dhnifu Bey, Herman & Michell Moncret, Phillip Mccain, Kenney Robinson, Earl Cobbs, Roy Jones, Charlie Brown Sr. Afred Young, Michael-Dennis-Melvin Johnson, Deadeye Heplin, Tony Moe, Bull & Box Bullock, Rudy More, Denise And Donna Walker, Sharon Young, Ronnie Jackson, Larry Mosely, Murrice Duckett, Mildred Ortiz, David Duke, and Ron Crockett.

Table of Contents

Introduction
CRIPPIN: THE EARLY DAYS

If the streets had won, this book would not exist. If I would have conformed to society's expectations of me, you would never hear this story. Instead, I won the battle, and beat all of those naysayers who would have wished to see me dead and buried or locked up for life. Rather, I am alive, thriving and can tell you my history. No child is born a gangster. But the circumstances presented in life and the folks in your world quickly shape the man you become. As I take you through this journey, you'll realize that the Crips did not make me who I am today. Rather, my roots and my upbringing led me to become a powerful leader of the Crips.

Looking back, I know my early notoriety in the streets shaped the leader I would become in California. My young victories were evidence that I could fight and would win. I watched my elders, and I learned fast from those who knew the game and came before. When many kids are just grasping hold of reading and writing, I was learning the rules of the streets. I knew how to be a fighter, and how to lead others with the respect I earned through my domination on those blocks. I never was a child in the true sense of child in the true sense of childhood. Instead of playing with blocks, I was running the blocks. Don't be fooled, like all youngsters it took me time to perfect my skills. But once I was good, I was unstoppable. Feeling that confidence and seeing how kids on the block followed me, even at a young age, created a foundation for me. I knew I was a leader from seven years old as I defeated my street rivals. Respect was earned and quickly gained as I created this rep for myself as someone to be feared in the neighborhood.

My story begins in the streets of Dayton, Ohio. For all you city folks, you may not think Dayton, Ohio and see gangs. But don't be fooled, the streets were hard. You had to be harder, or you got run over fast. From Dayton, Ohio to South Central Los Angeles, my evolution took shape. If I only knew as a youngster that my fight was just beginning and where each fight would lead me. My later domination of South Central Los Angeles and my role leading the Crips all came from my young lessons. My name, is Angelo "Barefoot Pookie" White. I was born to Charles A. White and Iva Jean White in October of 1956. Yep, so that makes me a true OG as I share this story with you, the story of my beginnings.

It was the early '60s, and while political leaders were fighting for Blacks to have equal rights in the US, I was fighting my own battles in the streets. We landed in South

Central during the post Martin Luther King Civil Rights Era. It was 1964 when I came to California. While Dr. King was fighting for a revolution in America, I began my own revolution in South Central. My family moved a lot. Luckily, I knew how to adapt and how to use my street skills. I had a knack for learning new neighborhoods fast and figuring out the codes of each new territory. As we moved from street gang hood to hood throughout the westside of South Central Los Angeles, to the eastside, to the northside, and then back again, I stepped up right where I left off in Dayton, and just kept swinging.

Chapter One
BUILDING BLOCKS

In 1963 before our family would migrate to Los Angeles, California at the age of barely 7 years old, I was initiated into my first street gang. We lived in the Soda Bass Courts in Dayton, Ohio. The city of Dayton at that time was about the same size as Pasadena, California for all you west coast people. It was close to nature, with lots of wooded areas just on the outskirts of the homes in the city. The woods were full of trails where you could explore, hunt, and fool around as a youngster. Dayton had some cold winters, too. I remember them vividly, because when you grow up poor, the winters are even colder. You don't have the right clothes to keep you warm during those winters, and they freeze you to the bone.

My Uncle Charles E. Burton, aka Barefoot Charlie, was the leader and founder of the project neighborhood street gang. Uncle Charlie was one of four siblings, and was the only boy in the group. My grandparents had first lived in Richmond, Kentucky. When they split up, my grandfather remarried Momma Lou, and they migrated to Detroit, Michigan to follow the jobs created in the car industry. My grandfather worked for General Motors, putting in long hours to get a taste of that American Dream. My grandmother was left with the four kids when my grandfather remarried, which was how she ended up migrating to Dayton, Ohio. In Dayton, she found herself raising four kids, one of whom was Uncle Charlie, in the Soda Bass Projects. The Soda Bass Projects were Black projects, and were the largest projects in Dayton, Ohio when she moved there.

Uncle Charlie found himself the lone male in a family full of females in a new rough area. Even as a 12 year old, my Uncle Charlie knew he had to step up and become the man of the family to look after all of the women, since my grandfather was not there. So, when a lot of young men are still enjoying youth, Uncle Charlie was taking the lead as the man of the house. Uncle Charlie quickly decided he needed to replace the void left by my grandfather, and made himself the man of the house. He learned how to street fight at a young age, having to protect himself and his family of all women.

Over time, Uncle Charlie became a reputable street fighter among his project peers. By 1959, he had risen to be the leader and found of the Soda Bass Courts Street Fighting Gang. When things got dangerous in the Soda Bass Courts, Unc struck back. His street gang was formed in reaction to a need for protection. The local street gang had taken hold in the hood, and people needed a way to fight back and to keep a hold on their homes.

As with most gangs, when people are in need of some resource to survive, they must gather and unite to find a way to meet those needs. It was more efficient to work together than to fight alone, so creating a gang was the answer. In the Soda Bass Courts, there was a need for power. There was a need to protect. There was a need to prosper. Just like the police claim to "protect and to serve," a street gang is no different. Just like the police, we were also selective about who we protected and what we served. It really is ironic how the police attack street gangs, when we really are all just operating with the same mentality. Protect ours and eliminate those who get in the way. We have more in common than people would think, but the difference is that one group needs resources, and one group has those resources.

My uncle's leadership in his street gang was something I admired. His power was noteworthy, and I saw the respect that his power got him from those around. We'd walk around the hood, and others would bow down to him. I wanted that same stature. Looking up to him as a young child, I learned that leading and protecting your hood got you respect. When a rival street game tried to take over our people and our resources, he fought back with his own street gang, and it worked.

When people threaten to break up your community, they start a war. Maybe they never knew the wrath would come, but when you challenge real men, they don't back down. They fight back and overcome. My uncle and his people were at war with this rival group that thought they could come in and take their women and break up their family unions. That kind of disrespect could not be ignored. Local gangs would come into the Soda Bass Projects to get at our females. Our females united the family union and held our families together. Trying to take that, tamper with that, or destroy that, meant war in the streets. Following our elders' lessons, I saw by the age of five that fighting was a must. There were a lot of kids my age and older in the neighborhood who were raised up knowing that fighting was just a necessary part of life.

There were other men in the picture briefly for me. My father, Charles Angelo White, was an Army war veteran who had served the country proudly and received an honorable discharge from the service. My father was a hard-working man. He and my mother were married for just 4 short years. From what I know, my father had over 21 children in his time on this Earth with at least 7 different women over the years. So you can see, he wasn't the love one-woman, stick around and raise a family kind of man. During the time my parents were together, they had my older brother, Chuck and me. It was just us two from their union. They moved the family to Cleveland, Ohio in 1956. I was born in October of that same year. By 1960, my parents had divorced. My mom relocated to live with her family, my grandma and Uncle Charlie, in the Soda Bass Courts. Since my dad was out of the picture by the time I was five, I soon turned to other men in the family to show me leadership and teach me the lessons of manhood. That's how Uncle Charlie became my mentor. The man I latched onto and admired from the age of 5 was my Uncle Charlie. He quickly took the place of my father in my life, filling the void as both father figure and mentor.

Those early days in Dayton were hard. My mom was doing her thing in the streets, and my grandmother was working two jobs, one full time job and another part time. I had aunties who lived close by in the neighborhood, so at least there were some supports when my mom was nowhere to be found. The women were doing their best to support us, and Uncle Charlie had stepped in as the male figure looking after everyone. I have traumatic memories of Cleveland that still haunt me to this day from my childhood. I remember my mother had left me for a couple of days all alone. The streets got ahold of my mom, and she wasn't always around. The place we were staying at the time was a rat infested apartment. I remember the fear of being alone by myself while rats of all size ran around that apartment ignoring my presence. It was like I was the visitor, and they were the residents, there were so many of them. I remember lying in the apartment in shock, unable to move as the rats ran around me like I was the one trespassing in their home. To this day, the psychological fear of being alone amongst those rats with no adults to go to for help still comes to mind. Trauma can do crazy things to a young child. It can make you or break you, and you have to fight hard to be sure you overcome those experiences.

Luckily my grandmother and aunties came looking for me after a couple days when they realized my mom has not returned. They rescued me from that terror. I truly knew the feeling of abandonment, though, in the days leading up to them coming, and it taught me that I had to fend for myself. If you cannot depend on your mom at the young age of 5, you go into a different kind of mindstate. You learn quickly to depend on yourself, first and foremost, and to look to those around you who are willing to lead you and teach you. Family becomes those who are loyal around you and who share similar struggles. When mom and dad are not the people you can trust to take care of you, others get their shot to be those people. For me, that was Uncle Charlie.

My Uncle Charlie was a fair skinned, nice looking, bow legged young man with curly hair. He had his pick of the pretty young ladies who were attracted to him. I always envied the attention he got from the ladies and looked forward to the day that I was the man they were all after. Uncle Charlie had a good heart, but he was a firm and hard leader in the streets. He got his pseudo name, Barefoot Charlie, from his escapes in the woods outside of Dayton. Uncle Charlie was notorious for running through the surrounding forested areas near our neighborhoods barefoot. It made him tougher. As youth, we would venture into the woods nearby our streets and use those wilderness adventures as our training grounds. We'd play fight, and challenge each other. Uncle Charlie would always look out for me. I remember, he often would carry me piggyback through the woods through rough terrain, around broken trees and even through areas where broken bottles scattered the forest floor. He did all that maneuvering barefoot and had immense toughness. That's how my Uncle Charlie's name evolved, and he became known as Barefoot Charlie.

From the young age of 5 years old, Uncle Charlie began teaching me how to fight and introduced me to his street fighting gang. The company of the members of the street gang gave me a group to depend on and to battle with against outside enemies from other territories.

It took a small village of relatives to raise me. I remember my aunties taking me in during times when my mom was gone and my grandmother was working. Walking home from school in the brutal Dayton, Ohio winter one day, I found myself totally alone and frozen to the bone. Being poor, I never had the proper clothes to stay truly warm in the cold winter wind, and that day the cold had won. By the time I made it to my apartment, I found a deserted home that was just as cold as the outside I had come from because there was no working heat. Feeling alone, frozen and deserted, as a young five year old walking home alone from kindergarten, I wondered what I would do to escape this cold loneliness of the Projects. I found rescue from my aunties once again, whose house I was up the hill and across the street from the Soda Bass Projects where I lived. My Aunt Chic and Uncle June took me in that day, no doubt rescuing me from what would have been a very long cold night. I remember Aunt Chic would often feed me and put me to bed. Those rescues I would never forget. Without them, I don't know how I would have survived some of those days alone. My aunties were some true blue real life Charlie's Angels! While those moments sure did toughen me up, they also reminded me that I was often alone. I had to make my own road and find ways to be safe and survive. Uncle Charlie's street gang would start teaching me more lessons about survival by 1963. That is when the humble beginnings of my street existence in Uncle Charlie's Soda Bass Courts Projects would take hold.

Chapter Two
EMERGENCE OF A WARRIOR

My earliest memories of Dayton life come in the vision of our old apartment. Back then, people burned their trash in steel drums behind the apartments. So, as I look back on that memory of Dayton, and my time there, the smell of the burning charcoal in those steel drums still overtakes my senses. My grandmother, Gracie May was the matriarch of the family. She was one tough cookie with a warrior spirit, and she was a force that could not be ignored. Some of my earliest examples of strength came from watching her deal with the harsh realities that came her way.

One memory rises to the surface of a time when Grandma and her second husband, Ike Clay, were fighting. We were all in a one bedroom apartment together those days, and my brother, mother and I shared the living room as our place to live. My grandmother and her husband were in their room when it began. All I know is my grandmother stabbed her husband, and all hell broke loose in those tight quarters! I remember the mad scramble to get him to the hospital from the wound she gave him. And before you judge, here's the backstory. My grandmother was a hard-working woman employed by whites as a maid. While my grandmother was working her fingers to the bone for white folks, her husband would sit on the couch all day, unemployed with his perfectly processed hair, thinking he was some kind of pimp. One day, she had enough of his lazy ways. They argued, and she stabbed him. As you can imagine, that was the end of that union, so we moved to the outskirts of the Soda Bass Projects to Lakeview, a place where my mom had been raised. During this period, I gravitated even further toward my Uncle Charlie as my role model.

Once allowed around Uncle Charlie's gang, it was clear that to get respect, I had to earn it. In the streets, you earn that respect through your actions, not words. There was no social media back then. There was no posting to the Gram or to the Book to show people your skills. There was no Snapchat or whatever new fancy technology all the youngsters use to brag about their exploits and victories at that time. Times were different. You had to rely on word of mouth to spread your rep around the streets. People came to know your name through the testimonies of those you had run through for good, or for bad. To earn your street degrees you had to face challenges and beat them down, literally.

I was initiated into the gang life by challenging and fighting against all the bad little boys my age. Once people saw my skills, they started to know my name. There's a saying, "You get further with fear than with love," and that's the truth. Nobody in the hood was gonna put me on a pedestal for being a nice guy. Nobody was going to look me in the eye, shake my hand, and open doors for me without me putting in work. I had to earn each street credential I got. Those small battles whooping up on the other fighters my age elevated my stature and perfected my game. I graduated from beating down the boys my age to embarrassing my older challengers. As I won fight after fight against those older kids, my power in the hood grew.

Our house was the gang's hangout. There was a lot of horse play and fighting between us as we prepared ourselves to defend our gang turf against outsiders. I had many fights as an initiation into my Uncle Charlie's gang. Just being his nephew was not enough for me to be initiated into his gang. Uncle Charlie made me put in work to earn my spot. There were a lot of horseplaying, too, amongst the gang peers in Uncle Charlie's gang early on. I came to realize that they were testing me and prepping me for later street fights we would face. Being with the gang peers was like being with a tribal community. We all looked after each other and our local surrounding neighborhoods, knowing that any threat to our people or our neighborhoods would lead us into battle. It was only after I had proven my strength and my loyalty to the group over and over again, that I could be initiated. So from the young age of seven, that was my focus.

What do other kids do at seven? I suppose they are just starting grade school, playing on monkey bars, telling kid jokes in the school yard, sounding out words and trying to learn some lessons in school. I suppose the toughest part of the day for some kids that age is the choice between PB and J or a turkey sandwich in their lunch sack. Daily, my decisions had to be sound because one wrong move could end my days. There was no room for playing around, no time to be a kid. I grew up fast. You have to when life is at stake. When you are a soldier at seven, your outlook on the day is completely different. Survival is your focus.

Uncle Charlie was a leader and a teacher by nature. Uncle Charlie brought unity to the neighborhood through his stern leadership style and his natural instinct for survival. In the summer of 1963, at 7 years old, under the tutelage of my mentor and father figure, Uncle Charlie, I was initiated into the Soda Bass Court Street Fighting arena. I had at least 30 fights with bad little dudes my size as my initial training regimen. Once I had worked my way successfully through those fights, I progressed to fighting older and bigger opponents. While I was battling my young way through the streets, Uncle Charlie was multi-tasking. He not only was leading the street gang, but he was finishing his high school diploma during those years.

That's one thing that always stuck out to me about Uncle Charlie. Here he was a leader in the streets, taking care of the women and looking after the safety of our neighborhoods, and all the while he was still going to school. Nowadays, gangsters drop out of high school because the streets take over their time and their focus. Somehow, Uncle Charlie still found a way to do both well. He truly was a leader in my book. By summer of 1963, Uncle Charlie had two degrees. He had his street degree, and his high school diploma. Uncle Charlie graduated from Dunbar High School in 1963. He enlisted in the U.S. Navy a year after graduation, in 1964, leaving me truly alone as my own man by the age of 7.

When we learned that Uncle Charlie would leave for the military, we held a going away party. Man, that was an epic night! I remember the party spilled outside of our house once the crowd got too big, and people were shaking a tale feather babe! It was off the wall! The party spilled into our front yard and into the streets as the Motown hits echoed through the streets and cascaded through the night air. All of the neighborhood and family friends danced through the streets to those Motown classics. We reveled in the voices of Diana Ross, The Supremes, The Four Tops, Barbara Lewis' "Hello

Stranger," Smokey Robinson, Little Stevie Wonder, and Martha and the Vandellas' "Dancing in the Streets." That was the night! We partied and danced until the sun came up. We didn't realize it at the time, but we were also saying our goodbyes to Dayton, and we were getting ready to head west.

With Uncle Charlie gone, my lessons came straight from the streets. My teachers were the big homies in Unc's gang. My Uncle Ronnie stepped in as the family leader once Uncle Charlie was gone. My Uncle Ronald H. Young Sr. had been stationed in the army base in San Diego, California while he was fighting for the country. He always had plans to return to California with his family after his time in the army was over. Uncle Ronnie was married to my mom's middle sister, my Aunt Bell. Their kids together were my cousins, Ronald H. Young, Jr., Rhonda, Carl and my youngest cousins Gary, and Lil Bobby.

With my new mentor, I listened close, and I watched closer. My mentors were my teachers, my disciplinarians, and my models for the future. I saw myself leading just like they led. I knew I could become even stronger and better than they were, just in my own right. Each small victory was like a block in building my eventual platform. Those blocks would lift me to my position in the future. Each opponent I conquered in those early fights got me one step closer to becoming that man who I looked up to and admired, Uncle

Charlie. He was the vision I saw in the back of my mind as I progressed from street test to street test. I saw myself becoming just like him as I got older and becoming a leader myself. My rep was taking shape in Dayton. I was becoming a young force to be reckoned with in the streets, but little did I know that Uncle Ronnie was going to shake up that foundation for all of us.

Uncle Ronnie convinced the family to make the move to California. He had been out west during his time in the military, and had vowed to return. So he convinced everyone to make the move with him and start over. On the day we were to leave Dayton, Ohio, a feeling came over me that was unfamiliar. My mind was racing back to the past, and my present seemed completely fake, foreign. I was sad to move from my early childhood roots which had been all I'd known. I remember a wave of emotions that filled my body as I thought about the move. Excited to see a new world outside of Dayton, I was also leaving behind so much! My mother had decided to stay behind in Dayton to pack up and sell any of the items we were leaving behind. The loneliness was once again staring me in the face. So, I was going it alone, no mom, no dad, just me and Ronnie and our extended family.

We boarded a plane to Los Angeles, my first time ever on a plane. That was a scary thing! To stay calm, all I could do was take myself back to those familiar and comforting

Motown hits ringing through my mind as I wondered about the battles that lay ahead of me. We arrived at Los Angeles International Airport around mid-day, I remember. My Aunt Belle drove us home from the airport in a black 1958 Chevrolet Convertible. She and my cousins were all in the car to take us to our new home from the airport that day. It was a blessed reunion to ride together with the sun shining down on us riding down Century Boulevard going east through the City of Inglewood. I remember feeling a sense of hope that things would be better in this new land, but in the back of my mind, I was prepared for the worst.

As we cruised through this foreign territory, I took in all of the sites. Palm trees, the sun beating down on our foreheads, the freeways. We arrived on 84th street and Figueroa between Hoover street, just minutes from the I-10 freeway, and I looked around me at the new streets I would call mine. Forced to grow up fast, my mom was not with me, and here I was in a new state with new rules. It was time to be my own man.

Chapter Three
STACKING AND REBUILDING

It was 1964 when we moved to Los Angeles, California. That was a time when lots of families were moving west from the middle parts of the country in hopes for a better life. There were promises of prosperity in the west and new industry. Not to mention the whole TV notion of California, and its job selling the dream of California to middle America. Families saw opportunity in a move. They hoped for better. In California, we did find opportunity, all right. Uncle Ronnie had his own vision of what California had to offer us. He had the military experience of Los Angeles when people took care of him and treated him with a certain level of respect based on his service to the country. However, once finished with his service, he was just another Black man embarking on the streets of Los Angeles with a dream.

Families in the south and Midwest had heard about job opportunities and a guarantee of prosperous living out west in the land of sunshine. Those in the military had gotten a small glimpse into the good parts of the west. LA had a strong economic base in agriculture, oil, tourism, real estate and movies back then. All of these industries were being advertised and sold to middle Americans and southerners as opportunities for a better life. LA grew rapidly with many suburban areas inside and outside the city limits. Hollywood had made the state famous, and World War II brought new industry, especially high-tech aircraft construction. Politically the city was still fairly conservative though. There was a weak labor union for all of those taking on blue collar jobs, which made it easier to take advantage of the new hungry families moving west. Sharks prey on the weak. Capitalism survives when there is a clear lower class of workers who will work low wage jobs. That's what the California industries were banking on with all of these new laborers flooding west for "opportunities."

We moved to south LA during a time when the city was undergoing major changes in their police force and the way crime was handled in the streets of LA. Political leaders in LA at the time, Fletcher Brown, and former LAPD detective Harry Raymond turned the tide in the city. In 1950, Willie H. Parker was sworn in as Chief of Police for LA. Parker pushed for more independence from political pressures and had goals to create a more "professional" police force. The public supported him and voted in changes that isolated the police department from the rest of government. Not realizing the effect that this could have, this additional isolation allowed the police force to work independently of outside regulations that created a lot of renegade officers who misused their power in the streets. Parker was ambitious. In a sense he created his own police gang by finding a way to function free of additional political oversight. Gangs operate off of power, control and often fear to protect resources. The LAPD were no different during this period.

The racial tensions spilled over into the police departments during the 60s. The races were geographically separated due to housing policies that allowed for segregation and gave tenants and landlords the right to refuse to sell or rent to Blacks. During the 1960s, the LAPD was promoted as one of the most effective police departments around the world, but I saw them at work first hand in our streets. And "effective" must have been a status given to them by those who didn't live in my neighborhood. They had an *effect*, all right, but not one that worked for *our* people.

Under this leadership and new vision for enforcement, I saw more and more police abuse of force and position. The tensions that came from these actions ended up resulting in the eventual Watts Riots of 1965 when people became so frustrated with the system that they put the city in flames. In August, 1965, the Watts Riots broke out. For you historians out there, you remember the devastation those Riots brought to the community and to local business owners. After six days of battling, the Riots left 32 dead, thousands of people injured and locked up and cost the city millions in property damage. According to later reports, the riot was a reaction to a long record of police brutality by the LAPD and other injustices suffered by Blacks, including discrimination in jobs, housing, and education. By 1960, Los Angeles had the fifth largest Black population in the United States, larger than any city in the South. Still, Blacks remained in segregated enclaves. With many of the high-paying industrial jobs gone by the time the 1960s arrived, Black unemployment was high. The growth of street gangs and drugs in the Black communities were a reaction to these problems.

So the fight did not change for me, it just got bigger. There was so much more at stake. Coming to California just before all of the tension exploded with the Watts Riots, what we found was a lot of the same. The setting had changed, but the streets were still the streets. There were palm trees instead of oaks. The cops wore black instead of blue. The street blocks were longer, the sun was warmer, and winter was really non-existent. But like any new territory, once you put a bunch of people in the same space with limited resources, fewer jobs, and the money is scarce, everyone starts fighting for more. And the beat goes on. The cycle continues, and the streets go right back to being the same battle ground. Different state, same battle.

In 1964, I had just turned 8. My mom did not make the trip to Los Angeles with us, initially, so I went west with my brother, grandmother, aunts and uncles. That was a surreal feeling, not having your mom around. But you make do, and you let the rest of the village raise you, until your mom can find her way back. I was beginning to understand the world and the people around me. I was starting to go through my own trials and tribulations. The little kids that I had close-encounters with were usually my neighbors. My intentions as a youth were good from the start as I started practicing my leadership skills. I suggested to the little kids I played with that they should join me as I read the Bible to them. Some came on board, and others laughed me off, but you see my intentions were good at the beginning. Those were the days of my humble beginnings in Los Angeles. I realize now that God's chosen people are called upon to practice his good will. Once I had my followers, we would head over to our neighborhood church together to surround ourselves in God's word. Our church at the time was Greater Bethany on the corner of Hoover and 84th Street. Bishop McMurray was our pastor, and his bellowing voice rang through our souls on Sundays as we cleansed ourselves in the spirt of Christ.

Though I didn't know that at 8, my intention to round up the local youth and lead them toward a greater good would always be a part of my being. I'm sure some would look back at my life and actions and question my intentions, but my vision was always for greater prosperity for my people. You see, I had a unique ability to easily transition from a leader in the streets fighting, to a leader who had a positive message to share with my peers. Looking back, that's what made me likeable. I had charisma and energy. Anyone can fake energy. But my charisma kept me focused on my vision for greatness, for a better way of life for my family. Others looked up to me for being strong enough to back up my words. But they also knew I was a child with faith in a bigger purpose for us all. I wanted to lead them to greatness.

After we had settled down in our new home in South Central Los Angeles, I was surrounded with both family and new friends. One of our first tests came from a neighborhood family named the Moodys. My little cousin, Little Ronnie, had complained to my brother, Chuckie, and I about this bigger boy who was trying to bully him. The bully's name was Donald Moody. Donald Moody was the oldest sibling of the Moody family. His siblings, Daryl, Dwynn, and their older sister, Denise Moody rounded out the Moody clan. Upon hearing the threat to our brother's safety, my brother, Chuckie, and I immediately went into fighter mode. We protected

32

family at all cost. Protecting each other was second nature, whether it was Dayton or Los Angeles. Family came first. Chuckie and I immediately took off on a mission to settle that conflict with the Moodys. We confronted Donald while we were outside on our block. After that first confrontation, we merged a bond with the Moodys that led us to be lifelong friends. Through that initial encounter our two families found respect for each other and became unified.

While I was getting my bearings in South Central, Uncle Charlie was still out fighting for the country from 1964-66. He eventually joined our family in California after leaving the military. Our family tried to establish a house painting business when we got to Los Angeles. Uncle Charlie gave that job a try for a couple years. But a tiger never forgets his stripes, and it wasn't long before he found himself back in familiar territory, the streets. The bright lights twinkling deceptively through the City of Angels came calling for my Uncle. He was just the first of many Black men to head that direction as we later witnessed. Unbeknownst to us when we set out for the land of prosperity in the west, we had actually come to Los Angeles just in time for the rise of many Los Angeles street gangs.

My family moved to 84th street between Figueroa and Hoover when we made our way to Cali. For those of you who don't know those streets, we were nowhere near the sandy beaches, sparkling ocean, and the wealthy mansions that were advertised in the media. There were family homes and apartments in this area, and the gangs had already claimed their roots. It was a Black neighborhood, and the options for growth did not match with what was advertised. Gangs had a stronghold on the area where I had come to call home. I was the newcomer. The new guy on the block was an unknown. Not like today, when you can flash your social media rep around, and suddenly your name is well-known by all the people around you, I had to rebuild *again*. Those foundational blocks I had started stacking up in the Dayton streets were still inside of me, but nobody could see my foundation. I had to start over from scratch, rebuild and demonstrate my strengths to those around me.

Some of the local neighborhood street gangs around me at that time were the Gladiators, Slauson Boys and the Businessmen. These were the notable and most popular street gangs in LA during the 1960's. My building blocks from Dayton came in handy when learning the codes of these new street gangs. The Hoover Groovers and Manchester Park Boys claimed and controlled the Hoover's local street gang neighborhood. Manchester Park and Bret Hart Junior High were the first South Central Los Angeles Elementary and Junior High schools in the areas controlled by those gangs. Principals and Superintendents like to think they control schools in the hood, but really the gangs had control. The school leaders were just figureheads riding the back of a tiger. At any time, the tiger could choose to buck off and run wild. As the 1950s and 60s Baby Boomers were trying to work for a better life, the street gangs were also booming and growing.

As predecessors, The Gladiators, Slausons and Business-men were the original street gangs that set the stage and established turf for the Hoovers street gang. As the youth grew in these street gangs, and evolved, so did the gangs. The Hoover Groovers and the Manchester Park Boys came next, and built up numbers which eventually led to the origination of the 1971-72 youth street gang, the Crips. Little did I know during my primary years, that I would become one of the most known leaders of what would become the Crips. But let's not get ahead of ourselves. I still had a lot of building that got me to rise to those eventual heights.

Angelo White

Chapter Four
MOBILIZING THE REVOLUTION

The area of Los Angeles named "South Central" was the only district in the city where Blacks could own property during a period of my youth. Racially restrictive housing covenants, enforced by the law, police authorities and white homeowners, kept L.A.'s schools and communities strictly segregated and denied many people of color the opportunity of home ownership. These biased policies led to the creation of housing projects. Initially, they were built for war industry employees, and planned with racial integration in mind, but they worked, instead, to segregate. Such projects began to populate the South L.A. neighborhood of Watts. Larger projects, such as Imperial Courts and Jordan Downs, which were built during the 1940s during WW2., also had a majority of Blacks living in them.

So, given all of that, having our own space and home at the time we came to LA was considered a supreme luxury. It was only possible because we had so many adults working together to support the home. But the homes were just a façade to placate us and make us believe we were making it. When the jobs were scarce and people around us started fighting each other to survive, those homes were just symbols of a dream that could not be fully attained without a fight and a lot of heartache.

Faith remained a grounding force for me as a young child. In 1964 before the Watts Riots of 1965, Vermont Boulevard was the market place for South Central Los Angeles communities. It was like the hub of the neighborhood, where everyone would come together. Some neighborhood kids and I would walk together to church each Sunday. One Sunday, our destination changed, though. Rather than heading straight to the church, as we usually did, we walked past the church on Hoover and ended our walk on Vermont where we found ourselves at the Thrifty's. Everyone scattered once inside, each going their own direction. I quickly understood that everyone had gone their own way in the store because they were stealing. In my mind, I knew it was wrong. I mean, here we all were supposed to be on our way to give thanks and praise, and instead we were in a store stealing. Rather than thinking for myself, I was caught up in the mob mentality of the escapade. I found myself in the middle of an act of sin and abomination when I should have been speaking the Word. This moment changed my Sundays from that day on. No longer would I venture to church with that group of kids for the kind of fellowship they wanted to enjoy. The following Sunday I opted to attend Bishop McMurray's sermon alone. A true leader knows when to walk away and venture out on his own. It takes much more strength to turn from a group than to follow the crowd, and I found that strength the next Sunday. I had decided that the group did not share my vision for success. I set out to The Temple of Greater Bethany in solitude, and I found myself reminiscing and missing the days back in Dayton, Ohio. This new group of Los Angeles neighborhood kids was just different. It would take some getting used to, and I was in the middle of that realization. After each church day, I would walk over to the Vermont Theater that they called the Badboy Show. There I would find other youth with similar interests. I found new avenues for unity with new neighborhood folks at that theater.

On Vermont, there were old school low riders parked and parading back and forth from Manchester Avenue down to Vermont. Before leaving the Badboy Theater, I stood for a second in the lobby of the show with the intention to leave and head home. While standing there, I witnessed an argument between two groups outside the theater. I noticed that one of the group of street gang fighters were all wearing starched Levi jeans with the left side of their pants leg cuffed up. Later on, I would come to know that group as the Slauson Boys.

Curiosity and my inner fighter instinct took hold of me, and instead of heading home, I followed the two groups to a vacant lot where they began to fight. Fighting in those days was different. We handled things with our fists and fought like true warriors. Nobody needed hardware to fight in those battles. We handled things face to face, man to man. As I walked home that day after watching the two groups battle it out against each other, I felt the joy and familiarity of home back in my soul for the first time. For some reason, seeing that battle renewed my spirit; it was familiar. Fighting, I knew; Los Angeles, I didn't. Making it home safely, I had a clearer vision for how life would change for me in Los Angeles.

It's funny how the people you meet end up shaping the paths you take in this journey we call life. In Cleveland, it was Uncle Charlie, my aunties and my grandmother looking out for me and teaching me those young lessons in survival. In South LA, some of my first neighbors, the Hardy family, had also moved from my hometown of Cleveland, Ohio. Their home became the hub of our activities soon after we all found out how much we had in common. Leroy and Martha Hardy came to LA during the Civil Rights Movement in the early 1960's just like my family. They came looking for better, but just found more of the same. Originally the family lived on the Eastside of South Central L.A. before moving to the

Westside 100's. Mrs. Hardy was our first hood mothers. The Hardy's house was our second home, on 113th and Denker Street. Her house was the hub where we would all gather to plan, plot and horseplay as we grew together as a young street force to be reckoned with. Our recruiting grounds for new members were our schools, and best believe, we had plenty of schools to recruit from in our youth. With how much we moved during my young years, there was no shortage of new ambition to embrace as I made friends and gained followers. We knew we could find lots of eager souls looking for protection and a family network in our classes in Los Angeles.

The Watts Riots of 1965 reminded everyone that racial tensions in Los Angeles had reached an all-time high. My church was a casualty of the riots, burning in the crossfire of fury and anger. Blacks were not going to sit idly by and put up with harsh living conditions, diminished work opportunities and impoverished neighborhoods for long. The period in L.A. was also known for being a time of "white flight." With more Black families migrating to South LA from the midwest and the south, there was an exiting of whites from those same neighborhoods. This "flight" led to much of South LA and the surrounding areas becoming mostly Black or Latino in population during the 60s and 70s. This also led to the some of the gangs beginning to fight each other. With whites leaving, territories became run by either Blacks or

Latinos, and conflict soon arose between various groups as they fought for control of the neighborhoods.

This was also the time of the Civil Rights Movement. Gang membership declined some during this period, as many former gang members became involved in a political and social fight, within the Civil Rights Movement. Many gang members joined organizations such as the Black Panther Party and the Brown Berets. These groups wanted Black and Brown communities to control businesses, employment, education, and the media in their area. They wanted to take back the streets from white people and white money. The Black Panther Party and the Brown Berets wanted to act as a community army, and organized people against police brutality and racism. A good example of this was Bunchy Carter, originally a member of a Slauson street gang. He became the leader of the Black Panther Party.

However, there was still a need to unite in my neighborhood. Whether the groups were fighting under the name "Black Panther Party" or the name of a local street game, the groups were looking for the same things. We wanted to hold onto our resources, and we wanted to live better. We wanted to support our families, and we wanted to be safe from outside enemies who posed a threat to our livelihood. In 1965, in the midst of the reaction to the signing of the Civil Rights Bill, came my first experience with Black uprising.

I remember the rise of white supremacy and oppression during that time of my youth, and man how it erupted that summer! It was the summer of 1965, and the summer Watts Festival at Will Rogers Park and Recreation Complex set the stage the Watts Summer Festival Riots. I remember South Central during the event and how the police jumped on a Black female which kicked off the reactions that led to a full day of rioting and protest. Blacks who had felt oppressed in racially secluded neighborhoods where they were not owners of the businesses around them, began vandalizing and looting public stores. The National Guard troops were brought in to handle the situation. The guards were posted everywhere, like toy soldiers trying to stop the masses of frustrated Blacks from expressing and acting on their pent up outrage. The troops actually slept on our front yards during these times in an effort to silence the storm that had been building up for years.

My grandmother Gracy Mae was caring for us still at this time. My mother had stayed back in Dayton, Ohio, and would join us later by 1965 with her cousin, Paul. Grandma had enrolled us in school and was our main caretaker during those times. I was in the 3rd grade at Manchester Ave, and I quickly jumped back in right where I left off back in Dayton. "Attended" is the key word. I wasn't necessarily there to learn my daily lessons in math, reading, science, and history, though I was no slouch as a student. I mainly attended school to create and design my own story and teach my own lessons. I attended school to recruit my own army and to take hold on my own new territory. In 3rd grade, I was the leader of my peers. I remember learning how to read and finishing my first book that year. It was a feeling of accomplishment, and though I had a mouthful of words I could easily share with others, it was a whole different feeling to be able to read the words of another person and see things through that person's eyes.

I would walk home from school with my brother, Chuckie, and my cousins Little Ronnie, Rhonda, Terry, Sherry, and Dundee. Dundee and I were in the same class together. I played some mean kickball, and would stay after school playing kickball. As we walked home, I would take notes of the older kids as they encountered each other and fought. The older kids would leave Bret Hart Junior High, and they would have to pass Manchester Park and Manchester Elementary on their way. One day the crowd of Bret Hart Middle School kids made their way to my kickball territory. I remember the shock in my body as I saw them coming my way. Though they likely had no intentions to try to fight me, that fighting instinct rose up in my spirit automatically as my mind dramatized the possible danger before me. Immediately, I found myself flashing back to my times in Dayton, Ohio and the street fights I dominated. In my mind, I played out all of the possibilities that could be approaching me, and I had my plan of attack ready to go, just in case. As they came by, I went into auto-pilot mode. It was a survival instinct to fight and to fight for self-preservation for me.

As an ambitious 3rd grader, I already knew how to fight and just needed to take on the new challengers in this new land they called the west. From my days involved in gang activities in Dayton, Ohio, I knew that I had the skills to take over my new schoolmates and my neighborhood. I claimed to be the King of the school from the fourth graders on down. I saw myself as the Principal of that campus, with all my classmates and the younger kids as my students. This outlook came from confidence. I had been challenged before, and I had the courage to come in and lead in a new setting.

Actions speak volumes, though, and I got to work quickly. I vividly remember another day after school on the playground at Manchester. I had grown bored playing kickball and channeled that boredom into ambition. I started seeking out campus opportunities to prove my domination. While preying around the campus searching for new challenges, I ran into an unexpected surprise. I ran up to a grown man, a custodian at the school. With my fast mouth, I started shooting and slanging my wild words his way. He didn't hesitate to react while I was talking all that mess, wolfing. He stole on me and caught me on my jaw with the quickness. This was a rude awakening for me. The streets came to me that day in school. That custodian threw that punch at me, as if I was a grown man. As I walked away from that punch, I thought to myself, "Thanks for the motivation, old man!" Though I may have been new to the challenges of L.A., I vowed to myself that he would be the last man who would disrespect me.

Chapter Five
STREET MERGERS AND ACQUISITIONS

Following the Watts Summer Riots, our families would all move to the upgraded communities on the Westside of South Central Los Angeles, known as Westmont. The area spanned from Vermont to Van Ness and Broadline. The territory ended at the City of Inglewood. At that time, Inglewood stretched from Van Ness to Imperial and Century Blvd North. My family moved right over to the Westside 100s territory. We were on Century Boulevard and Wilton. The Westside 100s were on 108th and Manhattan, just a few blocks away from our new landing spot.

In 1965, the Westmont Community was made up of a majority of white families. The schools in the neighborhood were Washington High School, Henry Clay Junior High and Century Park Elementary. I loved the neighborhood! Of course, our street conveniently fell just outside of the boundaries for the school district, though. We were able to get by without people noticing that we were using our Uncle

Ronnie and Aunt Belle's address for two semesters and sample the environment in those schools, though. I was in the 4th grade at Century Park Elementary School. Some of my lifelong friends came from my short-lived attendance at that school. Some of the trusted friends I met at that school are still my do or die friends to this day. Those who are still here with me today like O'Neal Brown, Darryl Butler, Darryl Armerlin, Michael Connalas, Carl, and of course, my older brother, Chuckie, all made those early school days in Los Angeles memorable. I even still run into some of my old enemies from those times, Curtis Marrow, AKA Original Buddha, who had transferred to Century Park from Manchester Elementary after moving into our new neighborhood.

That nickname was clearly not indicative of Curtis' outlook on life as a youngster. Buddha and I got into a conflict after he bullied my little cousin, Ronald. For Christmas that year, Ronnie had been given his first new bike. Buddha decided he wanted that bike, and took it. I remember following Buddha and finding him sitting on my cousin's bike, like he had always had that thing. I walked right up to him, punched him in the jaw and knocked him off that bike. He landed right on his butt. My cousin jumped right back on his bike, and we left for home. The situation reminds me of the old saying, "You always see somebody twice," as that

48

wasn't the end of my encounters with Buddha. One day at lunch time Buddha spotted me before I saw him coming. There was no small talk, and Buddha certainly didn't waste time trying to get his payback for that strikeout with the bike. By the time I saw him coming at me, the same way I had come at him, it was too late. The punches were frantic and already upon me. Buddha was motivated to get his swings in retribution for the initial embarrassment I handed him. He caught me with that element of surprise and rushed me with a combination of punches. My response and reflexes to defend the onslaught of punches he was throwing my way, finally kicked in, however. A true warrior does not stay down long, and is never beaten. I began fighting back, and we were a swarm of furious flinging arms for several minutes before school staff came to break up our battle. A teacher's assistant finally saw us and ended the chaos.

I wouldn't see Buddha again after that fight for the next 6 years. I'm guessing that fancy white school quickly gave him the boot after that display. Schools didn't waste time kicking out Black kids back then. If you were trouble, they showed you the door quickly. You found yourself on the receiving end of an "opportunity transfer" to another school in the neighborhood. The name itself is ironic. You were giving an opportunity to start over, but really the school was taking the opportunity to send you packing.

My departure wasn't too far behind, I came to find out. Those two semesters bought us some time living the good life in Century Park Elementary School, but things that are too good don't last too long. After my fight, the school quickly found a way to conduct an address check and found out that we were out of boundaries for that school. The jig was up! The school officials happily sent us packing after finding out about our fraudulent address on file. That led my brother and I to our forced enrollment at Manhattan Elementary School.

My mom also re-entered by life around that time and joined the family again. When my mother and my Uncle Paul finally arrived in LA driving that old raggedy '55 Chevrolet that never should have made it across all of those states, they were also hopeful for a fresh start. Looking back on their journey, I have no idea how they had made that ride. God must have been on their side, cuz that old car sure covered a ton of miles without much left under the engine. But my mom's heart was full when she finally arrived, and she believed L.A. would be a new beginning for everyone. Sometimes the powers that be take hold, and God sure must have been pushing that old Chevy to LA. I was sure happy we were finally reunited!

As a youngster, my lessons had already given me a foundation for my vision. I was primed to end up in that street gang evolution. As a new student at Manhattan Avenue

Elementary School, I got acclimated fast. Manhattan Elementary School was one block north of Century Boulevard behind Sportsman's Park and Recreation. The transfer to the new school was a hard pill for my brother and I to swallow initially. But we found a way to deal with it, and continue supporting each other with our brotherly love, sticking together through the changes. At my new school, my first challenge to fight came quickly. The battle was waged over a girl. Jackie Burkheart was my neighbors, and she lived around the corner from us on 103rd and Wilton. Jackie was my girlfriend, I *thought*. I came to find out Jackie had also made a boy at school, Anthony Soilier, her boyfriend. That Jackie! Who knew! Anthony was a member of the Sportsman's Park Boys. Sportsman Park was their neighborhood park turf, and it included the 90s neighborhood and the Manhattan Elementary School area.

There was never a face-to-face confrontation between Anthony and I before the KOs began. A few of the Sportsman Park Boys had approached me prior about my relationship with Jackie. I responded to them reluctantly, and had taken the questions and comments as jokes at the time. Of course they were jokes! Jackie was my girl, and I didn't have reason to think otherwise. Since I did not show fear with those initial efforts at questioning, I irritated the Sportsman Park Boys, and a battle was imminent. They had to fight me, as they felt I had disrespected them and laughed in their faces about a topic that was serious to them.

They challenged me to a fight after school one day as my brother and I were walking home. My brother and I had taken our usual route home, taking the trail through Sportsman Park, from the sidewalk trail, through the park sidewalk that was between Manhattan Elementary and the giant golf course. As we walked toward home, we sensed we were being followed. Once we reached the park we stopped our walk and turned to face the group of Manhattan Elementary kids that had gathered and was following us to fight. The Candidate brothers were leading the pack. The younger brother called me out to fight head up. Our punches continued all the way from the beginning of Sportsman Park to the park's exit. The younger Candidate was not much older than me, and he had the fury to battle that day. I had an arm reach advantage on him, though. He was strong and persistent and kept grabbing me and trying to pull me to the ground where we would end up grappling. My brother had to pull him off me a couple times so I could catch my breath. Once we reached Century Boulevard, a punch hit me from nowhere. I was knocked off guard, and I fell into the usually busy streets of Century Boulevard. I can only imagine what a spectacle we were to the passing cars on the boulevard that afternoon. Oh, that Jackie! Had I only known! Sometimes things are a curse and a blessing, though. I had my first solid opportunity to prove myself to the local gang opponents that day, and I held my own. They saw that I was no punk, and that I had some serious heart and would not give up a fight. Though ultimately defeated that, day, I battled hard, and I showed everyone I was not someone to be overlooked. The respect had been earned.

While at that school I met people who would become lifelong family and friends, also. Some of those that have lasted a lifetime are Curtis Brown, Carl Mosier, and my best friend, Rodney Jones. Rodney's dad was a Sergeant Rodney Jones of the Lennox Sheriff's Department. Rodney's brother was my idol. I admired his style at the time. He was the king of the school, and I regularly spent a lot of time with the family at their home. On weekends, we would kick back and listen to Sgt. Jones' jazz collection, and Rodney would spend the night at my house with my family. At that time, the Jones kids were not affiliated with the Sportsman Parkboys. Their only connection was that they shared the 90's neighborhood and the Sportsman Park Recreation area. I would never go back to Manhattan Elementary after that first Los Angeles defeat. The only thing that would give pardon to the memory of that defeat for me was payback and revenge.

We were raised to be warriors from a young age with the mentors around us showing us the way. I remember for a period of time in my early childhood, every Saturday all the young men of our family were participants of the U.S. organization. Ron Karanga was preparing us for the Revolution to come. We were being disciplined as young warriors. For hours we marched together in one of the vacant lots on Fig Street. Our boots were shined, and we we were suited and booted. Just like a gunslinger, I was going after every reputable rival gang member to fight, too, during this time. Bret Hart Junior High, and Manchester Park were the 1960's breeding grounds for what was to come in L.A., the imminent capital of street gang violence. Of course, I was tough at Manchester Avenue as the self-proclaimed leader of the 3rd graders on down. But I did not realize at the time that I would carry the king of the throne to the 6th grade at another school, 59th street elementary.

From the time I had been inside of L.A. it seemed like summer lasted forever. In the summer time in Ohio it sometime rained with the sun out shining. I did not have the slightest idea that one day I would become an original gang member and co-founder to one of the biggest gangs in America and abroad, but I knew I needed to bounce back from that defeat in the park.

Chapter Six
BATTLING AND DOMINATING

Flash forwarding a couple years. I had accepted and reveled in the fact that I was raised to be a fighter. Just like some kids are gifted in math or science, my strengths were leading others and fighting my challengers. The memory of that defeat motivated me and helped me stay focused on my vision for the upcoming years. All I had in my mind after that defeat was to get back to my natural environment and regain my reputation as a street gang fighter who all respected. The Powdrills' family came into my life around this time. Larry was the oldest, and then there was Ronnie, Kat, Rucelle, and the youngest brother, Beedee. Larry and Ronnie were a few years ahead of me in school, and I looked up to both of them. I admired their survival fighting skills. They were a force in the streets of Los Angeles. They had style, and gained a reputation as street fighters in the hood. Mrs. Powdrill was a beautiful Black woman, I remember, and their family became another group who I looked to for mentorship and camaraderie during those early days. She was an independent and hard-working mother, as she provided for her kids.

Ronald Powdrille and I became very close friends and road dogs. He was older than me, 13, and I was 10 at the time. Even with the age difference, we still rolled like brothers. I learned about many lessons in character and was inspired by Ronald during our friendship. Though Ronnie and I got separated for a time, I would run into him four years later.

When we reunited, I was about 14, and had become much wiser and experienced in the survival lessons of the streets. By that time in my young life, my mother had remarried. Her new husband was a man named Billy Greene, and from that time on, Chuckie and I would spend a lot of time relocating together. We must have covered much of the westside by the time I was 15. We relocated from house to house throughout all parts of south central Los Angeles. You could say, my fighting came in handy doing those periods. In all those moves, I had to restart each time. Stability and my mom were not intertwined. While with her, my brother and I did a lot of packing and a lot more starting over.

Nothing was stable, no constant school, no neighborhood norms, nothing. I was always adapting, changing, learning my new surroundings, and finding how to be stronger with each new move. I moved around as much as a military brat, but our war was the one being fought throughout Los Angeles in the

56

streets. We were the product of the adults trying to navigate those warring streets. In 1967, when my family was moving all over, we went from the Westmont area and began our journey through the westside of south central's neighborhoods, deeper north into south central's westside, and moved to 22st and Western across the street from Danny Grace Mansion. The neighborhood was called "Sugarhill District." My mother enrolled Chuckie and I in 22nd Street Elementary School. Keep in mind, we were *across* from the mansions, definitely not living in them. I still had to find my own way to take charge of my life. The view across the street of all of the wealth, though, was motivating. I could see nothing but the fruits of others' success and their wealth. The neighborhood was an estate of mansions. Marvin Gaye and his family, Danny Grace, and other famous folks all resided in the richer areas of what was known as the Sugarhill District.

At 22nd Street Elementary, my brother and I would experience being in a new school once again. We found ourselves learning the new environment and figuring out how to be strong in our new surroundings. I found one of my first jobs during that time selling the Herald Newspaper. On Sundays, I would rise as early at 3 a.m. when most of the drivers on the road were coming home drunk from partying the night before. I would ride my bike around the neighborhood, and throw my paper route out of my backpack.

I had to have a lot of courage at that time of the morning. The streets on each block looked like spooky mansions, and I found myself challenging my own fears each Sunday morning to make my first legit money. Though, the money didn't come fast, and sure wasn't easy, it was mine. I felt good about having a job I could call my own and a paycheck that I brought home. Relying on others was not something I could do with constant change all around me. I had to make my own any way I knew how, through self-preservation.

Chapter Seven
UNITING FOR THE CAUSE

In 1970s as the Black Panther Party and the Brown Berets began to dissolve, street gangs came back. The Bloods and the Crips quickly formed and made a name for themselves throughout Los Angeles. The Crips started off as having two sets, the East Side and the West Side. As America's economy shifted from an industrial and manufacturing base to the service sector, factories started to leave L.A., and job opportunities declined even more for Black workers. Around this time, there was also a greater movement of flight. White residents had been leaving for the suburbs, which added to the loss of revenue and business opportunities in South Central. The areas in South central entered a period of even greater economic hardship and financial struggle. Many black political leaders had been imprisoned or marginalized by that time, and Black youth in South Central found themselves left without role models in the community.

During this period, the number of street gangs increased. A gang called the Baby Avenues was started around this time by an ambitious 15 year old teen, Raymond Washington. At the tender age of 15 teen years old Raymond Lee Washington would claim a vacant throne and install himself as the leader of the Eastside Cribs. The original pronunciation for the street gang was changed by the Los Angeles news when the media misspelled the name for the first time in 1972. With that editing mistake, the notorious street gang name evolved from Cribs to Crips. The name would change again in 1972-73 becoming the CA---Crips.

That same year a movement that became known as The Crip Multiplication and Turf-off began. By that time, I had had become known in the streets as Barefoot Pookie. I enlisted my leadership skills and helped lead the multiplication efforts. Our original Westside Crips would expand and multiply into a new name, Turfs. As street gang leader within the Crips by that time, and known to all as Barefoot Pookie, I would support the legacy of Raymond Lee Washington who was known for the saying, "Chilly Chilly Bang Bang; Crips Don't Die They Multiply." The multiplication efforts focused on recruitment of youngsters looking for family and needing a cause toward which they could direct their anger. The gang would target and recruit young members into the "Crips," Community Revolution in Progress Servants.

By 1971, I had been affiliated with several westside neighborhood street fighting gangs. I made my way through various territories becoming a member of the 100s, the 80s, the 60 Avenues and the Westside Smaks through my youth. Moving from neighborhood to neighborhood with my family played a huge part in these affiliations. With each move, I had to find myself a new network. After a year of being actively involved in the transaction of the Crips Multiplication, I found myself facing new kinds of trouble.

One night after the Sportsman's Record Hop, real chaos threatened to break out between rival groups. There were close to 200 partying youths gathered to enjoy the night together, and at the end, violence erupted. The teens were in the streets, and I noticed some brewing tension between a crowd of mostly Crips. In the midst of the angry group, I spotted my childhood mentor, Ronnie Powdrille. He was in a heated argument and was edging toward Donald Archie AKA Sweetbacc and James Cunningham AKA Cuzz. I knew them as elders from the original westside street fighting gang from the 80's original westside neighborhood, which turned into the Crips territory in 1971 under the leadership of Big Stanley Williams and Donald Archie, AKA Sweetbacc. Seeing all of the major players involved, I rushed over to the group with the intention of breaking up the fight between my fellow Crips. Though Ronnie was not a Crip, he was one of the original reputable street fighters. I knew it was risky to jump in the middle of the beef, but Ronnie and his brother had mentored me from 10 years old, and I owed it to him to try to prevent the fight that was impending. So, at times, tensions even brewed within our group. It was up to us to control those tensions and stay united toward our greater goals of dominating our neighborhood. If we fell apart and battled each other, we weakened ourselves. We knew we had to unite for social change to occur.

My evolution of greater leadership in the Crip gang began in 1971 with the "Crips Conglomeration" with south central Raymond Lee Washington and his Eastside Cribs, stemming from the altercation we had with Westside Inglewood Crips. In 1972 Raymond Lee Washington was with the original Westside Crips and was convicted of a Crips murder that was an accident. I was just 14 teen years old when we joined the up with Raymond Lee Washington. Raymond and I became real tight up until the time he was convicted for that accidental murder. He would take me all on the Eastside, and I would introduce him to the Westside. He surprised me one day when he made the announcement to a gang of my friends on the Westside which included Linda Day, Sheryl Bradley, Sandra Ford, Sheryl Were and a host of other friends. That's when he made the surprise declaration that he and I were the leaders of the Cribs. It was determined that he would lead the East and I the Westside. This was later recalled and named the "Cribs Conglomeration" as the unification occurred between the East

62

and the West in an overall vision to take over the streets together.

Raymond and I became very close after the 1971 "Crip Conglomeration." I took him around the westside neighborhoods, introducing him to X Smak street gang members who had turned into original Westside Crips. I introduced him to my girlfriend Cheryl Bradley and her girlfriends. Soon after, there was a neighborhood gang conflict with the Westside Inglewood Crips and the Smak's. Raymond was called to handle the situation at the Rio Theater, which was the Westside Smak's hangout. The result was the decision for the Smak's to join up with Raymond Washington's notorious Crip gang. We decided to meet the following Monday at Washington High School for the, "Westside and the Eastside Crips Conglomeration." Before the meeting was over we chose Larry Powdrill as the leader of the new original Westside Crips. Larry had led a fearless group of street gang fighters when I was just in elementary school growing up. Larry and his crew were vicious street fighters in the hood. Featuring the likes of big Steven Good who for the exception of a powerful looking body he was handsome enough to look like a playboy type. Steven Good was known to beat down more than one due at a time. Ronald Bennett had huge hands and not only would he fight as long as it took to beat you down, he would prey on street fighters none affiliated in the hood or out who were reputable. Ronald Powdrill Larry's brother next to his age was kind of quiet but with squabbles. Jimmy Johnson was two time light heavyweight golden glove champions who turned street fighter. These elder no name street gang fighters in the rich rolling 100 neighborhood during the mid-late 1960's were the vanguards that influenced the coming of the Smak's and original Westside Crips. Their reputation had grown respectfully through their street gang activities they protected their hood. In 1969 they were known for responding to a neighborhood squabble and turning on Washington High's entire football team.

In 1972 after Raymond was convicted, I initiated and became co-founder of the Crips Multiplication and Turf-off on the Westside original Crips turf local and abroad, with a new name the Westside Crip Hood. It wasn't too long after that night, that I found myself accused of murdering a rival street gang member. At the young age of 15, I was charged, convicted and sent to juvenile detention. While locked up in that boys' facility for six months, I went back to some of the strongholds of my youth, my faith in God and the words in the Bible. Nobody can describe the hell that one deals with in a youth detention center in Los Angeles. There are notorious stories of physical abuse that are allowed to occur between those walls. Really, those facilities are just a breeding ground for creating a stronger warrior or for breaking down those who never belonged on the battle field in the first place. If you don't get tougher in those facilities, they eat you up and can destroy you. It's a me or you mentality in those facilities, and I had to endure and overcome that time as a young teen for the street life I led.

I found myself looking to the Bible for solace and peace during that time of solitude. Who knew that my young childhood exploits in Dayton, Ohio and our training grounds in those streets would lead me to what I had become? Trauma takes a toll on a kid, though. Looking back, I know that's clear, if nothing else. I would be in and out of juvenile detention during much of what should have been the rest of my youth in various boys' facilities during my teens. At the age of 19, I was released and returned back to continue my path in the streets of Los Angeles.

When I arrived home, I picked up right where I left off. You see, there's no kind of *rehabilitation* that occurs in a juvenile facility. You either become a stronger version of what you already were, or you deteriorate. I just got more resilient. I read a lot, and I became more determined to return to the streets and lead the Crips toward more dominance. What doesn't kill you, just makes you stronger, and that's what happened to me during my time locked up as a youth. We decided we were going to defend the Hoover Street Crips that were coming across Vermont, heading west into our original Westside Crip hood trying to overtake our original Westside neighborhood turf. I was 19 teen years old at the time. My childhood had disappeared over a decade ago by that time, and I had been leading my own charge as a man in charge of my own destiny.

After 5 years of being an original member of the Westside Crips, I had survived being shot three times and had survived my stint in juvenile detention. I also had survived what probably could have been a fatal wound in the belly. I took a deadly stab with a knife while street fighting. Picking up right where I left off, I found myself disciplining a newly named Turf member in the City of Long Beach.

My return to the streets of L.A. coincided with the Palladium murder involving major original adult Crips gang members. So, needless to say, I returned to a lot of tension and heat in the community. People were out for revenge and payback. I moved back in my original hood and turf, the Westside 100's on 107th Street between Western and Denker. Without real formal education due to my constant moves from school to school, the streets and my street mentors had taught me all of my life lessons up to that point.

Every day we had been posted up on 107th at the Young's house and my house. We were discussing the original borderline of our original Westside turfs, an issue with the local street gangs surrounding our original Westside Crips Turf. We were natural enemies with the outer hood neighborhood street gangs. The Athens Park boys and the Denver Lanes were two of our original street gang rivals. The Inglewood Families street gangs were originally the Inglewood Chain Gangs, thronged by Big Tank and the Inglewood Chain Gangs. The preceding two original rival gangs would become and call themselves Bloods, eventually. Our two gangs would wage war against each other throughout the streets of L.A. for the next decade, battling for control of territory and the economic resources that came with those territories. I would be right in the front lines of the war, leading the charge.

Epilogue
LEADING CHANGE

I can look back on those younger days of my life with a greater understanding of my actions and my role in society. Growing up poor, you constantly seek a better life. You want more for yourselves and for your family members. When wealth surrounds you but is just out of reach, young people look to other means to get the things they desire. When the youth feel powerless in society, they seek that power. They hunger that power, and will sacrifice everything to get that control back in their lives.

My family structure was fragmented. I was raised through the consorted efforts of so many loved ones who worked together to bring me along, teach me lessons and try to mold me into a man. My Uncle Charlie helped me evolve into a warrior. The women in my family did their best to keep me safe and give me shelter during some of the hardest times in my youth. Uncle Charlie taught me the street lessons and strengthened my skills to lead. He introduced me to the gang life, too.

Trauma is a powerful force in a young man's life. When you grow up seeing violence, death, and destruction all around you, it does something to your insides, to your soul. You have to find a deeper strength from within to overcome the horrors around you. So you fight. You fight with all you have to be better and to be in power. You lead others in your battle to be greater and to overcome the economic and societal forces that seem insurmountable.

Much of this was what inspired me and led me to be the man I have become. Like I said, it's a wonder that I am even alive today to tell this story and to recount the young battles that shaped the leader who eventually lead the Crip gang into some of the harshest battles in California. No man is an army, though, and I always knew that was true. I could lead, and I always knew that others would follow.

Looking back, much of the time we were fighting each other when we should have been fighting others. We should have focused all of that anger at the people who created the economic hardships and states of desperation in which we lived. We lost a lot of brothers in our street struggles. Some are locked up to this day. Others have gone on to their judgments with the Lord.

If there are overarching messages I want to share from those times, it would be to remind you of just three things. You must first know what it is you are fighting for. Secondly, you must know how to unite with others to fight alongside you in your quest to find justice and to overcome the injustices that surround you in this world. Lastly, you must act, and you must be united in those actions.

Through your actions, you may lose loved ones along the way. You may even lose a bit of yourself, at times. For us, we knew our goal. I knew that I could not fight my battle alone, as it was never just *my* battle. And so *we* acted; *we* fought. My battle was just getting momentum in my teens, and the war waged on for many years thereafter. For those continuing the battle today, the revolution is still very real, and through any war there will always be casualties.

PHOTO GALLERY

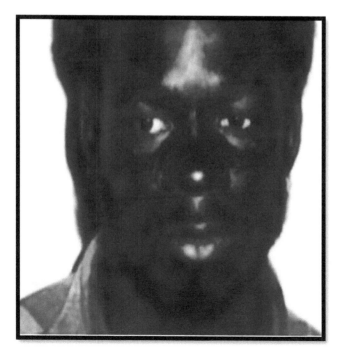

"*Make It Last Forever*"
Prom 2007

Printed in the USA
CPSIA information can be obtained
at www.ICGtesting.com
LVHW070812091123
763293LV00031B/7

* 9 7 8 1 9 4 5 1 0 2 4 3 1 *